ODE DU JOUR

Volume 1

Fifty odes for Everyone

by

Peter J Lyons

Observations from an enthusiastic spectator
and occasional participant

ISBN   978-1-9162208-0-5

Published by Town Clock Books
Printed and bound by SRP Limited Exeter Devon

Author's Introduction

Welcome! I hope that this volume will bring
you enjoyment and even at times spark an
emotional response. The odes are inspired by
imagination, topical happenings and
occasionally by a strongly held view. I imagine the
latter is more likely to evoke a positive response:
if not agreement, perhaps food for thought!
A few dates appear. Generally they fix the ode
into the timeframe of the event to which it responds.
If you enjoy this volume there are others.

☙

**Dedicated to Rosemarie my wife for
her unfailing support**

Index

"Yes, me too. I'm really looking forward to reading them. They say he's quite entertaining!"

"I do hope so!"

"By the way, he does his own illustrations".

"How interesting!"

Time Zones

(for the frequent flyers)

I find it is a tad confusing,
fly off West into the Sun,
you fly for hours and hours and hours,
and arrive before your day's begun.

If you could get aboard a rocket,
and take that self-same flight,
it would be even more alarming
'cos you'd arrive when it's still last night.

Travelling East is not much better,
for the Orientals are cunning you see.
No matter how fast your transport
the clocks always seem ahead of we.

Hold hard it's even more confusing,
for if to the East you seriously haste,
somewhere off the coast of Australia,
you find you have a whole day to waste.

No wonder the body's bewildered
and barely knows which way is up.
It thinks it knows it's Thursday,
but which week is just down to luck.

Harvest Time

(for all food producers)

Harvest Time's a time for rejoicing
when all is gathered in.
It's always considered late Summer
a'fore the festivities can begin.

But now we've all gone global,
let's stop and give a thought,
for in some far flung corner
each day's Harvest of some sort.

Just look at supermarkets,
strawberries at Christmas time
and how did the folks in Chile
give us melons oh so fine?

New spuds flown in from Egypt,
Moroccan this and that,
exotic fruits out of our season,
it's like delving in the magician's hat.

We've lost some of the excitement
of seeing the first crop of the season.
But I guess we've now reached a point
and have luxuries without good reason.

But don't forget the British producers,
especially the farming folk,
who toil out in all weathers,
at times it's really no joke.

So when it comes to our Harvest Time,
let's pay it more concern,
for in a state of emergency
it would be to Farmers that we turn.

Of food programmes on the telly,
there are more than several score,
but do the masses cook for themselves?
You're joking. 'Oh, Pizzaman's at the door!'

But wait, 'We need a new kitchen'
we oft hear young house buyers declare.
But what the hell do they do in them?
Certainly not their family food prepare.

When Harvest Time comes in due season,
or when you're buying at the Deli,
keep the home-grown grub high on the list
for it's surely best for everyone's belly.

Loyalty

(for the dog lovers)

Black and white name of Nel ,
a feisty bitch as ol' Bob could tell.
To the trials field she'd never ever been
but had she set paw, she'd have been the Queen.

From the break of dawn
to the setting of the sun
out on the wild moor
they worked as one.

Nel quickly learned the ways of ol' Bob,
and always did such a wonderful job.
She learned all the sounds of his demands
and oft was way ahead of unspoken commands.

That fateful day she was on top form
when ol' Bob fell, in a heap forlorn.
She barked and tugged and licked his face
but poor ol' Bob just lay there in that place.

Nel knew he needed help, that terrible day
and leaving the flock, she was off and away.
At the farmhouse door she created such a fuss
that the missus tumbled it meant 'Come wi' us.'

Gwen grabbed her phone and left her place,
Nel ran ahead, at far too great a pace.
Gwen knew roughly where ol' Bob would be
and then heard Nel, who now she could see.

Once at his side, his state was clear
and young Nel came over and lay very near.
The helicopter noise was a big surprise
as it lifted Bob and Gwen, up into the skies.

Nel knew that now she was on duty
and stood proudly there, in all her beauty.
She instinctively collected the scattered flock
that the copter had caused to run amok.

Poor Bob didn't make it, and sadly now is gone,
and Gwen and her son just have to soldier on.
Young Nel at the funeral suddenly appeared
and lay there a crying, as the coffin disappeared.

The Wind is in the West

(for the marine historians and all Westcountry men)

The wind is in the West me boys.
The tide is running high.
Tis time to haul the anchor up
and let the foresa'l fly.
We're off to rout the Spaniards
who dare to threaten we.
They clearly think they have a plan,
us knows not what it be.
We'll sail across their bows me boys
and not across their stern.
We'll sink them Spanish galleons
a'fore they'm time to turn.

"We'll need to come upon 'em fast
a'fore they know we're there!"
T'was Bob the powder monkey,
the son of Tom Adair.
His first time into battle
and ready for his war,
but a'fore the day is over
he'll be a boy no more.
The clouds came in with thunder,
rain, 'eavy as could be,
but up there in the topsa'l
Jan calls "they're on the lee".

Cap'n Drake he gives the order
and we set to cut 'em off,
and sink they Spaniards quickly,
and do a proper job.
The night was long and bloody,
all fighting for our lives,
and many a maid was widowed
beneath those angry skies.
But rout the fleet we did me boys
and saw them off for good.
And those that missed their wettin'
ran a'fore the wind, that could.

So us bold boys from in the West
did save old England's day,
And oft this famous tale's bin told
with a hip, hip, hip, hurray!

Modern Commerce

(for the home builders)

Buzz buzz went the chain saw.
Crash crash went the tree.
Chug chug went the tractor
and broom broom, the big lorry.

Zing zing went the bandsaw.
Thud thud the pieces fell.
Bang bang went the hammer,
another chair to sell.

Ding ding went the cash till.
Pop Pop the car arrived.
Clap clap went the children,
as they got the chairs inside.

Thud thud went the table mats.
Ring ring went the spoons.
Chink chink went the glasses,
to toast their new heirlooms.

🍎

Balance

(for the privately educated)

He'd never even tried it
and he knew it was a dare.
But he had to go one better
than that kid with curly hair.

The other boys were jeering
and keen to egg him on.
In truth he was just petrified
for it could go so wrong.

The pole had been first added
to fly flags on special days.
No fixings were provided
and the pole had dodgy stays.

At right angles the pole protruded
from the second storey roof.
Crawl to the end and back again,
of courage it was proof.

'Aloft' the cry would echo round,
when new boys would be tested.
The challenge had been strongly banned
when one youngster had protested.

So now in strictest secrecy
the tradition still survives
and seeks to force the new boys
to risk their poor young lives.

John thought to go one better
and set the end to walk.
There was a sudden stunned silence
and not a soul dare talk.

He stretched his arms out from his side
and focussed out ahead.
At the end he slowly turned around
and came back safe, not dead.

A cheer rang out across the quad
they slapped his little back.
Of genuine admiration
there surely was no lack.

John took the praise with dignity,
tears almost in his eyes.
In truth he knew he'd do it
so for him not much surprise.

For him it was quite simply
the height above the ground.
He'd walked on many a narrow ledge,
in fact all that he found.

Tree boughs, walls and railings,
railway lines and all,
but not like this latest challenge
with such an almighty fall.

Overnight he became a hero,
the pride of the lower thirds,
until the Head called John in
to have a few stern words.

John went in rather meekly
and took the reprimand.
The Head himself an old boy
was secretly quite charmed.

Much later John became Head Boy,
the gift lay with the Head.
John set to end the practice
that for years filled him with dread.

The pole he sought to get removed,
to hell with old traditions.
The Head agreed the pole should go,
no need for long petitions.

Crystal Ball Gazing

(for all forward thinking citizens)

Look very very closely
into the crystal ball.
Scroll on and on and on,
if you want to discover all.

Try stopping for a closer look
at year twenty two and twenty.
Surprises you'll find there,
be assured there are aplenty.

You'll find that all the human race
is nowhere to be found,
but robotkind both large and small,
across the world abound.

A few humans did escape, 'tis said,
to live up in the stars.
Some even took up residence
up there on planet Mars.

Most of mankind across the world
went out with all the nukes,
but just a few hung on, they say,
in spite of Trump's rebukes.

The problems all stemmed, you see,
from man's lack of humility.
The last have long since passed away,
having succumbed to gross obesity.

The flora and the fauna
have taken back the earth.
The robots they are working
for all their cells are worth.

They need no food to nourish them,
they're fed by tide, wind, sun,
and run around quite naked.
Seems they are having so much fun.

Deserts are receding
and grass long since reached the Mall.
In Germany all the *Stadts*
can scarce be seen at all.

Animals roam freely
across the new lush plain.
There are also brand new creatures,
the robots have yet to name.

Trees sprang up, across the globe,
CO_2 rates they have fallen.
Most of man's plundering
will soon have been forgotten.

There are the odd skyscrapers
that have not yet quite collapsed,
but if you look more closely,
you'll see they're full of cats.

The earth is in the robots' hands.
They're doing quite a job.
They're cleaning up what mankind left.
'Oh my', he was a slob.

The robots are creative.
They built a mountain range.
It's made of plastic they collected.
How's that for being strange?

Robots can be so clever,
they keep finding brand new ways.
They get the job done personally,
and no other robot pays.

But they have not tried to launch yet
any new kind of religion.
Rejoice, for there need be no Wars
or other kinds of division.

It seems to be going so swimmingly
out there in twenty two twenty.
But wait, what's this that I can see,
surely it's a mistaken entry?

It looks just like a problem.
What a thing to set before us.
Oh God, how sad, all robots dead,
wiped out by a computer virus.

Technology

(for the philosophers)

Do you ever watch those chimpanzees
and their clever use of sticks,
or how they open nuts with ease?
Oh they're such clever-dicks.

Why would we be surprised then,
if their successors, yes mankind,
should always want to find the fix
that leaves the rest behind?

Cave woman gave to us the wheel.
Egyptians dealt with their mummies.
Stonehenge got its planning through.
China's gunpowder was not funny.

On and on the inventions grew,
man's talents oh so mixed.
There were so many great benefits.
In diverse fields they fell betwixt.

T'was oft that War seemed to be the driver,
as man strove on to become the survivor.
So many a brainwave proved the saviour,
while others came by chance or by man's labour.

Of industrial revolutions
we've oft been known to speak,
but surely the last century
is actually quite unique.

The so called great progress,
moved on at such a pace,
some even began to wonder
if it helped the human race.

So many changes we have experienced
since the end of World War 2.
Car journeys replacing bus rides,
and two-car households quickly grew.

Pressure cookers and smart phones,
even automatic mowing,
and on Continental holidays
the masses now regularly going.

But it's perhaps computers
that now do rule the waves
and slavishly fix life's pattern
from our cradles to our graves.

We loyally talk to strange voices
recorded in places afar,
who cannot answer questions,
and care even less who we are.

Kids used to chat and dash about
when they were all let out,
but now they walk like zombies,
heads down, one thumb stuck out.

The smartphone now possesses them
and rules their poor young lives,
ruled by what other kids have texted
and published up there in the skies.

There is no doubt that the Internet
can be a force for good,
when it's used intelligently,
as surely that it always should.

It can answer most questions
and be a force for learning
but, we know there are bad things too,
and hours and hours are burning.

It's said that finally the body
will make dramatic changes.
Unused limbs will wither, and fall
into rivers from mountain ranges.

Thumbs will grow grotesquely crook'd,
other fingers will just merge,
ears will come with earphones
to let perpetual Pop be heard.

Eventually technology
will seek to conquer all.
Reality's already a thing that's fading,
and one day soon will take a fall.

We'll expect to print new body parts,
just at the drop of a hat.
Travel? Press a button. Be transported.
So what do you think of that?

It won't be like it use-ter was,
somehow we have less hours,
but think of your ancestors.
Were their times worse than ours?

These changes, as they come,
and come they will for sure,
so chin up, chest out, be brave,
and try texting that Bank once more.

Responsibility

(for all that volunteer)

ANYBODY could do it,
SOMEBODY surely would,
NOBODY actually did It,
NOBODY felt good.

SOMEBODY regretted it,
ANYBODY could see,
NOBODY even noticed,
but EVERYBODY was peeved.

SOMEBODY reacted,
ANYBODY could see,
NOBODY seemed to notice,
SOMEBODY was relieved.

EVERYBODY gave a shrug,
ANYBODY could see,
Seen his sons like this before,
So he climbed the stair, back to his bed
To snore again some more.

(*did you find the twist? Did 'it' get done?*)

Responsibility

(This may help if you missed it!)

JOHN could do it,
FREDDIE surely would,
BOB actually did It,
BOB felt good.

FREDDIE regretted it,
JOHN could see,
BOB even noticed,
but DADDY was peeved.

FREDDIE reacted,
JOHN could see,
BOB seemed to notice,
FREDDIE was relieved.

DADDY gave a shrug,
JOHN could see,
Seen his sons like this before,
So he climbed the stair, back to his bed,
To snore again some more.

ఔ

English

(for all English speakers)

Out of the mouths of British folk
come words by the score,
and it matters very little,
if we're rich or if we're poor.

Each and every one of us
use many words each day,
even those that are not quick
to insist they have their say.

But try to get them speaking
in someone else's tongue,
you might as well be trying
for Mr Micawber to have some fun.

They think that English serves them
and covers all their needs,
but little do they realise,
their tongue comes in all breeds.

Over centuries in the past,
new words have been included,
brought to this pleasant land
by invaders and those befriended.

Ready to come tumbling out,
we store words of great mystery.
One doubts that many recognise
their mouths are full of history.

We started with just Celtic words
but soon we added Roman.
Will the Conk brought us the French,
then we got some from our foemen.

We sailed the seas both East and West,
seafarers learned a few,
then came the Europeans,
from States both old and new.

When Brits went off to conflict,
to fight in many wars,
they brought words from India,
and a couple from the Boers.

English is a mongrel,
but gives speech its potential,
So those that shun the foreign tongue
find it inconsequential.

The joke of course lies in the fact
so many do not see,
without our Greek and Latin base,
English might not even be.

There's ne'er the slightest interest,
in a word's derivation,
those Brits just chatter on and on,
with words from every nation.

The Music Makers

(for everyone who thinks it's them)

Just how and when it started
no one really knows,
but one thing that's for certain,
it preceded West End shows.

It might have been cave person,
who noticed clanking bones,
or it could have been a sailor,
who heard the rigging's tones.

Then of course we realised
noise of fauna does abound,
so it's hardly that surprising,
that man chose to add his sound.

No doubt there were experiments,
and tests of every kind,
then banging, blowing, shouting,
were progressively refined.

Egyptian hieroglyphics
give hints of instruments past.
We surely know for certain
Romans had horns on which to blast.

It can be well imagined,
man soon learnt a song to sing,
at war to keep his spirits up
or when gin down throats they fling.

As part of the refinements,
music was to be written down.
Now there's a thought to conjure with,
it took men of some renown.

All those dots and squiggles
chopped up in things called bars,
no wonder they needed tonic,
to go with their sol-fahs.

They finally came together,
those that writ and played and sung,
classical music was created,
entertainment had begun.

Man is so creative
and soon spotted there was a need
and soon was into madrigals
and a wider use of reed.

Not all could be participants
in this upper-class kind of thing,
so they invented folk and country
so the peasants too could sing.

Instruments moved on as well.
Keyboards were invented.
Wind and brass followed on;
progress ne'er relented.

Music in all its formats
soon crossed all national borders.
Kings and Queens commissioned
composers with countless orders.

Soon most people were taking part,
from singing round the fire
to making music in many ways,
even singing in a choir.

Orchestras were founded.
Opera came closely on their heels
and lesser grade musicians,
sung and played at people's meals.

Music became so popular
Promoters entered on the scene,
so many gave music a whirl,
but found they were soon has-been.

Music is just everywhere,
in pub and clubs and cars,
if truth be known there can be few
who can say that music jars.

You can afford to pick and choose.
Good music always survives.
So go along and take *your* pick,
music *will* enrich your lives.

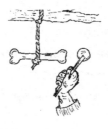

The Queue

(for those that only stand and wait)

Strange that we adopted
a French word with such meaning,
to represent a practice here
some regard as so demeaning.

In France a queue is quite different
but I doubt you care a fig.
It's a knot of hair that adorns
the rear of a gent's periwig.

This little word for us describes
how chaos becomes good order,
queuing is a National trait
little found outside our border.

It started way back God knows when,
a form of polite behaviour,
most foreigners don't have a word,
for they crowd and give no favour.

In World War 2 you prowled the streets,
yes looking for a queue.
It signalled that food had arrived,
what kind no one actually knew.

You joined quite rightly at the back
and grasped your ration book,
you shuffled forward hope in heart
it would prove something to cook.

We queue for buses and for trains.
Usually in abject silence
but let someone get out of line,
well just occasionally there's violence.

At football and the January sale
where we queue with one accord,
regardless of the activity
just hoping that we've scored.

There is one other country
to which queuing's been exported.
In the USA they stand *In Line*,
now our success has been reported.

In regulated activities
queuing is catching on
so on the whole it's good for us,
so let the queues go on and on and on.

Little words can mean so much

(for those of a linguistic bent)

English is a language
more difficult than some.
Its richness of expression
comes from sources more than one.

We've adopted bits and pieces,
from friends and from our foes
and produced a rich amalgam,
that can decorate our prose.

I ask that you consider
this word that I have chosen,
for it illustrates most perfectly
words have meanings by the dozen.

The word of choice is whip,
a strange choice I will agree
but by the end of this small ode,
you'll surely think like me.

Our first thought could for instance
be old coachman, whip and horse,
but it could so easily be
just whipping up a mousse.

Politicians not to be left out
have adopted the little word too,
they use the word so perfectly
to tell MPs what they must do.

In hotel kitchens large and small
chefs of each and every gender,
whip with hoots of great delight
and shun the mechanical blender.

Sailors say they are whipping
when rope ends they are fixing,
while burglars also use our word
but for them it just means snitching.

The list goes on relentlessly.
It once was used as punishment.
Golfers speak of whippy clubs,
sportsmen of sudden movement.

Some say it is what you do
to get things back in order.
If you've just thought of another,
'Sorry I've switched off the recorder'.

so ah do no in
at be or of me
ah to if is

H$_2$O

(for us all and the flora and fauna)

This mix of alpha numeric
as seen written up above,
is a scientific formula
and one we should grow to love.

If man only had the ability,
we'd roll about with laughter,
we'd mix oxygen with hydrogen
and end up with lots of water.

It's not just a lovely liquid
with which to wash, drink and play,
it is the essential element
which all life needs every day.

It's always been so important
to find and protect resources,
regardless of whether
for man, woman, child, plant or horses.

It was once said by a professor
that water upon this earth,
was an ever constant volume
whether found above or below its girth.

True or not is of no import,
not for the likes of we,
but it is quite essential
when we set out to make our tea.

That's actually being quite trivial,
for in places beneath the sun,
the constant search for life's elixir
is certainly not much fun.

In realms close to regions polar,
rain sometimes exceeds our need.
But there between, in the tropics
you can barely grow a seed.

Bore holes and artesian wells,
reservoirs and dams,
are but a few of the initiatives
that man's search for water spans.

One thing is quite certain,
we need to protect this gift
and try to use it wisely,
or into deserts we could drift.

World Peace

(for the diplomatists)

Now here's a thought to consider
and *thought* is the operative word.
I want to look at World Peace
if that doesn't seem too absurd.

Whenever we open our mouths to speak
behind it there lies a thought
and if your language has no word for it,
chance of communication is quite fraught.

We've invented misunderstanding
for situations such as these
but in the final reckoning
it can produce desperately bad deeds.

So how do we solve this issue,
and ensure complete understanding?
To see there's a word for each thought
may only be achieved, by the last man standing.

Better by far to tackle head on
this complex diplomatic disadvantage,
there is just perhaps only one way,
we must use just one common language.

That in itself could so easily lead
to conflict or great conflagrations,
so we'll soldier on to keep the peace,
until English becomes used by all Nations.

Who is a Winner?

(for achievers great and small)

O.K. so let's for starters
accept the true facts of life.
We are not all born equal
so don't try to give me strife.

Let's look at this another way
and search out the smallest talent,
then build on that just bit by bit
an approach that's much more gallant.

If you can only spot it
and quickly help its nurturing,
I doubt that there is one of us
who can't achieve things heartening.

The secret lies in gentle help
and love and patience aplenty,
then tiny talents will surely grow
so giving all a point of entry.

For some with special aptitude
if the right help they can enlist,
they are the ones most likely
to become life's gold medallists.

Yes there will always be a few
who've been dealt a rotten hand,
but with our help, gifts oh so small
can grow as most understand.

Like great oaks grow from acorns
and for man the odds may be thinner,
but still each talent can also grow
and become in its way a winner.

The Coconut

(For the ornithologists)

If you're old like me
you'll remember the day
when tropical fruits
never ever came our way.

Now there is so little,
that evades the busy shopper.
'Cos somewhere in the world
everything's a current cropper.

I have in my mind
that large brown nut,
we first met at the fairground
in the 'Coconut Shy' hut.

It all seemed so romantic then
as they came from tropic strands,
to end their ever sunny days
in shy winners' eager hands.

Then there came that time,
not so very long ago,
when we shared it with the birds,
perhaps something you already know.

They seemed to enjoy it
for them t'was something new,
but as the years rolled on
far fewer joined the queue.

As the economy developed
feeding birds became the norm.
It quickly became the fashion
to put food out on the lawn.

Then there came a change,
bird food became a passion.
Proffered coconut was rejected,
quite clearly out of fashion.

We can surely now predict,
with some degree of certainty,
if you offer coconut today
and despite your regularity,
our little feathered friends
will reject it day by day.
Hopefully they'll not grow obese
if on designer food they stay.

It

(for all those that think they have it)

I've never even seen it
However did you miss it?
France asked to import it
Spain would not release it
Germany said they'd tax it
Denmark said they dropped it
Italy said they'd got it
Russia's not sure about it
USA have banned it
Britain did once have it
Acid rain just dissolved it
So now nobody's got it

Did *you* get it?

ⓒ

A Square Meal

(for those that toil in the kitchen)

In English there is a scattering
of little words we always link.
We use them all from day to day
but of their source we never think.

Now what about *a square meal?*
We usually just mean there's plenty.
In fact it's quite historic
and been around since thirteen twenty.

In older times the gentry
almost always had a plate.
But poor folk from their tables
directly with fingers have ate.

They oh so wished a plate they had
but were forced to improvise.
They came up with a canny scheme
and bits of bread were their surprise.

So of bread they took a nice thick slice.
They placed it on their tables
and piled their food upon it high
no need for accompanying bagels.

No table linen to be soiled
no washing up as well,
not quite like Kings and Queens and Dukes,
on table manners we'll not dwell.

The *square meal* became so popular
we've heard tales that are Teutonic,
and even now in the Fatherland
they take bread and place food upon it.

There is one other benefit
from those early times we glean,
at end of meal, just eat your plate
and leave the kitchen clean.

From the Soapbox

(for supporters of free speech)

The seed is standing ready.
One day it's fertilised.
The worldwide number's heady
as dreams are realised.

After initial reaction,
the belly starts to swell,
just time for some reflection
then life starts with a yell.

If you reach 80 long years
and you've learnt much on the way,
this ode seems quite fortuitous
for the poet to have his say.

Life comes with pre-built qualities
from deep within D – N – A
that also gives life some certainties,
but there's still much for which to play.

The race is on, the time is short,
basic principles to instil.
Our early training we must sort
lest all else go down hill.

Within but days the newling
will have sussed what gets results
and plays one off agin another
and ignores the mild rebukes.

What'ere new law facilitates
set down by liberal thinkers,
the babes need learn from partnerships
of parents from both genders.

'Tis vital that they live and learn
from parents within their homes.
Farming out to nurseries
will risk producing drones.

The foundation of a loving home
and guidance Mums and Dads provide,
will make schooling productive
and protect life's bumpy ride.

Without a good foundation
real teachers don't stand a chance,
and progress through the system
won't their futures much enhance.

And talking of that system,
that Politicians love to change,
it really is so simple,
why why can they not engage?

Without a grasp of the three R's
broad based learning can't depart.
So if parents fail to do their bit
where can formal education start?

The one fundamental error,
(my opinion if I may),
is to believe we are all equal.
Not so, for ever and a day.

The overriding policy,
indeed perhaps a creed,
is to give the child opportunity
at levels where they may succeed.

We've become obsessed with human rights
to embrace things we have listed,
areas where equality of personal success,
could never have existed.

One of life's important lessons
everybody just has to learn,
is to cope with occasional failure,
that's life, smile, 'til it becomes your turn.

Time to stop just kidding
and give the child a true fair chance
to fulfil their actual potential
and not falsely their achievements enhance.

So stop teaching except in English,
address language in pre-school,
match pupils' potential to facility
let that become the golden rule.

A University education
ain't a universal panacea,
especially with exams dumbed down,
so fail? oh no, not never.

Get the platform right with 3 R's,
stream according to ability,
sort academics from the practical,
restore a true sense of reality.

Any sense of failure will evaporate.
Happiness will return.
The Nation will be rewarded
for once a lesson will actually have been learned.

Let the Politicians claim the credit,
they'll do it anyway,
but this independent Nation
will live to fight another day.

Carpe Diem

(for all opportunists)

The world's full of opportunities
but seen by only some.
The trick of course is timing,
to grab them when they come.

It may be in one's childhood,
seeing the value of education,
or perhaps upon the sports field
when you run with such elation.

It's all about awareness,
interpretation of conditions.
To see the chance and take it
so not just of pre-planned missions.

Old countrymen had a saying
that fits the bill so well.
It said, *see a stick and cut it*,
come the next no one can tell.

So as we travel on in life
be aware of each of these chances.
'Grasp the moment' eagerly,
so health, wealth and happiness advances.

The Establishment

(for all rate payers and voters)

Why ever did **they** do it?
It really is a mess.
You'd have thought **they** surely saw it,
I'm speechless I confess.

Again **they** failed to deliver.
They are a rotten crowd.
Of course *we* can do nothing
but just rant and speak out loud.

I read it in the paper.
They are doing it again.
We all know so much better
and **they** never take the blame.

They say they'll learn the lessons.
But do **they**?, hell as like.
In no time flat it happens again
and no one's told, 'Get on your bike'.

But stop, should *we* be helping?
They're only human after all.
Should *we* muck in and give a hand?
Oh no, that's not our call.

They have all the resources.
They have cushy jobs you see.
They really are responsible,
it's nothing to do with **me**!

High Tide

(for all who sail the ocean blue)

If you're not a regular yachtsman
and you don't swim in the briny sea,
or trawl for fish for a living,
of tide times you have little need.

You go through life oblivious
of the power of the ocean blue,
and disregard its clever motion
all recorded to give sailors a clue.

The tide rolls in and then pauses,
it's governed by the moon they say.
It stands, and then the flow reverses
and it happens twice every day.

Not quite the end of the story
for the moon plays other tricks,
some days it lets tides go further,
both near, far and betwixt.

At the expense of irritation
I'm afraid it don't stop there,
for the times change, yes daily,
please don't tell me you just don't care.

The tide's developed a vocabulary,
so seafarers can keep things short.
If you're in a bit of a quandary
you don't have time for a long report.

When marks of High and Low waters,
closest one to the other creep,
it's according to the moon's phases
and they call these tides a Neap.

At times the boot's on the other foot
and the moon its influence brings,
when high and low are far apart,
now they say these are the Springs.

When the tide rolls in with foam topped waves
that reach way up upon the strand,
a'fore it rolls back out again
they say the tide is on the Stand.

The receding tide gently starts to Ebb,
the waters on their journey go,
and across on other far beaches,
their high tide starts to Flow.

So thanks to the old Man in the Moon
we have this wondrous action
and folks go miles and miles and miles,
to witness earth's greatest attraction.

The Gap Year

(for those that lack a plan)

Now here's a modern invention,
symbol of the decadence it breeds.
Sadly a mark of self-indulgence
when youngsters have no economic needs.

I know, you are affronted,
how dare we speak thus of your son?
Well actually also of your daughter
for her gap year's already just begun.

The case I offer is quite simple.
Surely by eighteen you know your mind.
The race is to the swiftest,
can you actually afford to be behind?

We hear of the good works you plan.
While others just the world will roam.
Is this really properly thought out?
We bet one day you'll also want a home.

When that time comes we wonder
will we hear how hard 'tis for you?
How *they* are not helping all young people
who claim rights they have to pursue?

Yes it's difficult we grant you,
but not impossible please God.
In truth it isn't really that different
so examine it, not dismiss the poor old ...chap!

The fundamental difference,
lies in life's considered essentials.
In truth they too have not changed
but been augmented by wrong credentials.

Here's a few that didn't feature
when we aspired to own our home,
we had no car, no fridge, no shower,
not even our own home phone.

As to the property mortgage,
the lenders had rules that were tougher,
just one salary was considered
and three times that became the offer.

Yes by all means add one's savings,
after all, we earned three fifty pound a *year*.
We cut our coat according to our cloth
and dismissed anything too dear.

We started at the bottom.
Upon the bottom rung.
With interest at seventeen percent,
'No', it was not always that much fun.

But our homes were a priority.
We did only what we could afford.
No one chose heavy credit then,
such mill stones were so abhorred.

One day we bought a telly,
later came a little fridge.
Our bikes had become a scooter,
still living on the garden veg.

Children came, God bless them.
Their needs were satisfied.
We had no smartphones or computers.
We talked, had fun, more than just survived.

By middle age we had moved on.
With no change in strategy,
we climbed on up the ladder,
even added, what we saw as luxury.

It perhaps is just this simple.
It's a free choice for us all.
We each need see our priorities,
in the end it's always just our call.

There is no moral to this small ode,
except perhaps just to say,
Gap Years surely have no place
if you really want everything today.

The Mason

(for all true craftsmen and craftswomen)

One of the World's enduring materials
adds strength, beauty and relief.
When worked by those that have true skills,
stone endures beyond belief.

Whether dry and out there on our moors,
or squared for buildings grand,
it also has the great properties,
to be worked by the craftsman's hand.

For walling there is no true substitute,
regardless of building styles.
Its use goes back for centuries
and e'en yet the eye beguiles.

We see it in ancient structures.
In cathedrals with mighty towers.
In gardens and the farmyard,
where e'er Masons display their powers.

It makes such great monuments
with fine carving quite superb,
for figures and depictions,
of no better material we've heard.

But with craftsmanship so fine,
that true masons oft exhibit,
with chisel and flashing mallet
there is virtually no limit.

Entente cordiale

(for those that actually care)

At first we thought it a glamorous drink
then a foreign welcome came to mind.
Finally we had a full description
from a linguist oh so kind.

Apparently it's from the French,
made to engender a feeling special.
One that links two great nations
across the narrow English Channel.

I wonder if that spirit will survive
as Brexit is fully rolled out
and will we hang on to the friendship?
Likely only time will remove any doubt.

Nidifugous

(for those with get-up and go)

The birds have been doing it for centuries
and beasts of every kind,
but it took till the twentieth century
for it to afflict the young of mankind.

There are two sides of each argument.
So we'll ignore the right and wrong,
cos actually it no longer much matters,
For most kids have become hangers on.

The Driving Lesson

(for all knights of the road)

All her life she'd seen the monsters
rushing here and rushing there,
she'd ridden in them regularly,
thus far without one care.

Then one day her Mum suggested
the time had perhaps come,
to acquire the skill of driving,
as befits most everyone.

Her immediate reaction,
was one of great surprise,
for never had she imagined,
her secret dream she'd realise.

Dad said that he'd be the tutor
and they'd use the family car.
He said he felt quite confident,
soon she would be fit to travel far.

They climbed into the monster,
wow, so different in the driving seat.
If she could get the training over
then her life would be complete.

She looked down in the corner,
there were pedals in a row so neat.
She counted them, oh horror!
Too many for her little feet.

Dad said she must not worry,
for they needed just the one.
Well occasionally we may need two,
but to gear changing we've yet to come.

Then there were all the switches
and dials set in a row,
and what's this knob in the middle,
surely not there just for show?

A mirror for your make up,
more mirrors on the outside,
a seat belt and a handbrake.
Fear swept in like a tide.

Dad told her not to worry
it's just a usual reaction,
for when first training is imparted,
most feel their brain in contraction.

They started with the many switches
and revealed the question of selection.
He explained the dials are advisory,
of Lesson One t'was a mere fraction.

They looked into the mirrors,
checked on the driver's door.
Wiggled the gear selector.
Glanced at the feet down on the floor.

Seat belts are all fastened.
Her fears were mostly gone.
Dad seemed quite delighted.
Lesson Two they'd switch it on.

Pond Life

(for the naturalists)

No, not that term derogatory,
used by lesser folk than we,
we mean those creatures aquatic,
that are such a joy to see.

You dig a hole there in the ground,
fill it with fresh tap water.
Then buy a few red goldfish,
probably a few more than you oughter.

As time goes by the water greens,
a frog chances it to find.
Gradually it clears again
as plant life too survives.

Then one day comes the frogspawn.
It sits there in great blobs.
A newt drops in and sets up home,
quite happy to share the grubs.

The odd toad comes to visit.
Birds drink at the water's edge.
It's all looking quite poetic,
till the Heron comes on long legs.

Alas alack the fish no more,
the frog has gone to hide,
the newts still seem quite happy
in the depleted pond to reside.

Hatches, Matches and Despatches

(for everyone)

This fascinating journalistic term
covers life from cradle to the grave.
The copy may be short or sometimes long,
but the printed version many folks will save.

The Hatches tell the interesting story,
of babes only recently arrived.
Their names and perhaps their birth weight,
but of bouncing we're never sure who tried.

A big stride in life's exciting journey,
neatly brings us to the blushing bride
and how on Saturday she was married,
perhaps the bump no longer could they hide?

The last of these three metaphors with meaning
is by far the very saddest of the three.
It speaks of the dear departed
and what they have meant to thee and me.

Churchmen have a similar saying,
used for those whose faith's not worth confessing.
Wheeled Christians describes the three brief visits,
when non-believers need the Church's blessing.

Reflections

(for those that remember their travels)

It's occasionally nice to reminisce,
to consider things from your past.
Some things that were actually quite serious
and others that now seem rather daft.

One theme keeps running through my brain
no need for lost memories to pull,
I was journeying in western Turkey
and en route to Istanbul.

He sat in the carriage corner,
with his forbidding staring eyes.
It was perhaps his crimson hair,
that had been the initial surprise.

I tried to engage in conversation
but he just stared with hypnotic eyes,
I averted my gaze as perhaps one would,
but could not avoid his tattooed thighs.

As the train sped on across Turkey,
the lad rose up from his seat,
stepped out into the humid corridor
and through our window displayed his feet.

They too had lots of tattoos blue,
even soles seemed to have their share.
I was alarmed just for a few moments,
that he'd re-enter the compartment quite bare.

Having completed his little demonstration
of strange manner and bodily adornments,
he donned a yellow ski hat
and ate sandwiches and other little oddments.

He settled with a sense of satisfaction.
Hurray! tranquillity at last.
He slept just like a small baby
all thanks to his fine repast.

In all my many Euro travels,
some great, and a few small disappointments,
that strange encounter was most certainly
more memorable than my Istanbul appointments!

Research

(for those who prefer facts to be facts)

Some speak without a thought of thinking
whether what they will say is quite right,
especially most any type of politician
who comes upon an opportunistic sound bite.

In truth most profess research to embrace,
some even have their own small crews,
but when that opportunity presents itself
they gush, though really have few clues.

Step up all ye bold researchers,
enlighten the ignorant with the truth.
Oh it must be so disheartening
to hear the boss make it up on the hoof.

This unfortuitous behaviour
is not the preserve of those upon their feet.
Lots of other types of communicators
are just as guilty when they bleat.

Short stories have their weaknesses,
novels, verse and other prose,
research, e'en just a tiny bit
would stop things getting up a reader's nose.

Research is a much broader subject,
permeating most any field you name.
It's through dedicated researchers' application
that so many wonderful advances came.

It's really the quiet patient people
sitting working in library and lab,
who use even best aspects of the internet,
and logic to discover solutions fab.

Never knock the studious researcher
prepared to work year after year.
Repeating, proving and recording
until new and wondrous answers appear.

Statues

(for those that have figured it out)

What is it that so encourages
those of questionable artistic bent,
to seek to produce graven images
of most anything man or heaven sent?

Depictions of the human form,
all sexes, poses and in several sizes,
some richly clothed in flowing robes
but mostly wear the smallest of disguises.

Scenes from most famous battles
and animals usually go down well.
Some pretentious oft noted proponents
produce featureless bronzes to sell.

Beauty is in the eye of the beholder,
at least 'tis what we've understood.
So it's for us in the final analysis
and I personally prefer mine in wood.

In modern times technology
has broadened sculptors' potential base,
reconstituted stone and resin,
have each now found they have a place.

For many when you say sculpture
they think of their garden gnomes.
It's not that they lack imagination
just they've visited no stately homes.

Fred and Aida visit quite regularly.
They regard it as a wonderful treat.
They alight there in the car park,
but discover it's not actually Longleat.

Most have heard of Moore and Hepworth,
a few of Edwin Landseer as well,
but 'twas Botticelli in his paintings,
that showed best how bosoms can swell.

The days when statues all wore fig leaves
to protect a few aspects from our view,
have more or less departed
unless the mallet and the chisel still hew.

It's a bit sad that such proliferation
of poorly crafted ill formed moulding,
has invaded retail's market places,
but better that than cultural withholding.

One thing mass markets do engender,
more want to get in on the act,
so the amateur sculptural fraternity
will grow and that's a fact.

Bath Night

(for the social historians)

A strong sense of anticipation
filled the house each Friday night.
For to bathe on any other day
would never have seemed quite right.

The bath hung on the kitchen door
with its supercilious galvanised grin,
it would have been some years hence
when we recognised it was just a big tin.

Large saucepan and a big bright kettle,
sat steaming, quite ready for to pour,
'O.K. kids get all your clothes off
I'll go and shut the outside door'.

Mum supervised the bathing order,
children were the first to climb right in.
Once dried and despatched to the bedroom
then Mum her own ablutions did begin.

And finally it was Dad's turn,
we think Mum always scrubbed his back.
He always got a warm top up
before the old tin bath went back.

Diphthongs

(for the elocutionists)

We recently decided to take up singing.
Made enquiries about existing local choirs.
We made our choice and soon discovered
the standards to which our group aspires.

T'was then we heard the rumour
of some strange infectious malaise,
we heard whispers in the tea break
about a Tenor having had his days.

The conductor made but oblique reference,
but it had clearly hit the Altos too,
oh my, had we made a big error?
It sounded worse than the Asian flu.

Next rehearsal in the tea break,
we gathered another crumb-like clue.
A Soprano let slip the full title
dip something but that's all we knew.

Attendance seemed to be steady,
clearly the singers were fighting back.
Less mention of the strange illness,
but of facts there still seemed a lack.

It was at the next rehearsal
that the whole truth finally emerged.
The Conductor at the end of his tether
used the mysterious term they'd heard.

The word it proved to be diphthong,
not an illness of any kind.
But for singers a serious problem
and one best left well behind.

Having hammered home his message,
the choir responded in their next song,
which was actually quite fortuitous,
for it contained not a single diphthong.

If you are actually an elocutionist,
then what you're thinking could be right,
but actually not on this occasion
cos they were just humming, O.K? Good night.

The Spring

(for those who are not quite sure)

When deciding upon a title
for my next outrageous ode
it was the view from the back window
that set me off down a confused road.

For it came to mind quite suddenly
that you might not think as me
and get fixed in your imagination,
some other meaning, 'cos there are three.

Of course I was thinking of the time
when nature comes back to life.
When trees and shrubs are clothed in green
and when most fauna seek a wife.

You could also easily be forgiven,
for imagining spring water as it thrusts,
with liquid that bubbles up continuously
from beneath earth's pervious crust.

Once again you might just have wondered
if I refer to that sudden reaction,
when animals and things move so quickly
as though released from some hidden traction.

Just one other small consideration
and that is the ubiquitous springs,
that drive the clock or reduce the shock
and do, oh so many other things.

In choosing such a common title,
(by the way the count's now up to four)
I've also started to confuse myself
so I guess the Spring I'll just ignore.

The Hat

(for all milliners)

He got a lead role in a G & S operetta.
One he'd never heard before he got his score.
The First Lord of the Admiralty no less,
he could hardly have expected any more.

Finding a costume was his responsibility
he set forth some ideas to unearth.
Found much sewing was most likely,
he'd be sewing gold braid for all he's worth.

Settling on a fine formal regalia,
that First Lords seemed to sport around
he set about designing a naval uniform,
but alas needed a bicorne hat he found.

Always ready for an intellectual challenge
he thought how it might best be achieved,
'I'll make one in my spare time', he said,
'so the Conductor's not too aggrieved'.

He collected an assortment of materials.
The black fabric made his little heart rejoice.
But the baseball cap and a Nissan brochure
might seem to some a strange choice.

The large pieces of dense polystyrene
might not seem to go so well with hair.
But with deft use of a Stanley knife
of sides he carved a rather fine pair.

He even used some wood screws.
Now who would ever imagine that.
But when all the bits came together
well it looked just like a bicorne hat!

With nimble fingers and small stitches
the fabric was progressively applied.
At last the hat was considered finished,
but for heaven's sake don't look inside.

The final step was the cockade.
White feathers adorning the crown.
Let's hope the audience is appreciative
when HMS Pinafore comes to town.

Paraskevikatriaphobis

(for all those afflicted by this)

I find this long word quite forbidding
and I don't even know what it means.
A mate tried to tell me but he mumbled,
all I caught was that it's to do with your genes.

They say it's to do with the calendar,
so I know it's somehow linked to time,
but if we've even got the right subject,
our search we will have to refine.

Eureka I'm feeling like Archimedes,
a bit more of the story I've found.
It seems it defines special people,
who fear when this day comes around.

So we've narrowed the hunt quite dramatically,
we're down to three sixty and five,
we've also been told there are not many
so our search seems to be still alive.

We feel we are getting much closer.
Plans devious have brought their reward.
Our clock man confidently assures us
Fridays will definitely strike a good chord.

So we've narrowed the hunt even further,
we're down to well under three score.
One more push for the final linkage
and we'll crack it before it's a bore.

Yes eventually we did finally get there.
We confirmed it's a Friday that counts
and the thirteenth day of the calendar,
when for some a great fear mounts.

Altogether not a nice feeling,
by Thursday you're filling with dread,
what to do when the thirteenth is Friday?
We suggest you stay safely in bed.

Holding on or letting go

(for the insecure)

It's usually just a question
of picking the appropriate time,
but for some it will be more difficult
for it involves their dream sublime.

It doesn't have to be romantic
but it's often about other folk,
sometimes it's about principles,
but it's seldom ever a joke.

You may try to seek consolation
from others who understand the cause,
but no one can truly substitute,
because the decision must only be yours.

The more difficult of decisions,
come when it's down to passing time
and the changing of normal standards
that with your principles don't chime.

Do you stand on ground you cherish
or do you elect to go with the flow?
The going can become tough for some
but in truth you just don't know.

It's a problem that besets mankind
as generations move steadily onward.
Each feels they must make a contribution,
believing each too is moving forward.

'Tis said if it ain't broke don't fix it.
But tinkering with things few can resist.
Perhaps especially our politicians
who from change-making will ne'er desist.

There are a few dramatic conditions,
when our theme has a serious deep feeling.
Hanging by finger tips on a rock face,
takes on a life threatening serious meaning.

It's not to belittle other situations,
but mankind to exaggerate is inclined.
But today's crisis may change perspective,
when later you pause and look behind.

So there I guess you have it,
do we hold on or do we let go?
Sure always give due consideration
but don't ever react just for show.

Stick by your guiding principles,
live your life by your chosen code.
Don't be a dog in a manger
but above all try never to explode.

The Copy Reader

(for the publishing professionals)

Now here's a sadly ignored profession.
One that gets far too little recognition.
The Gals and Guys behind the scenes,
spend hours correcting the authors' submission.

Those authors may have their good points,
like plots and characters galore,
but that clever turn of phrase falters
if the grammar's just like grade four.

You've missed another full stop!
Typed three instead of thee.
Left out all commas completely,
split infinitives throughout Hee, Hee!

But here they come to the rescue
complete with red marker pen.
They knock your text back into shape,
you win best author yet agen.

You quite forget to thank them,
well they're just doing their job.
The author always takes the credit,
Copy Readers just get their three bob.

The Punt

(for scholars, scullers and others)

You must surely have seen them on telly,
or perhaps from the banks of the Cam.
Occasionally there are just so many,
it resembles a bad traffic jam.

I speak of course as you've tumbled,
about the ubiquitous punt.
So beloved by the many bold scholars,
always well prepared for a great shunt.

The freshers all step up with boldness,
leap into this vessel not stable.
Some quickly find that they're swimming,
while others find to balance they are able.

It was all about creating an impression,
upon that young woman with blue hair,
he met her at a scientific lecture,
but sad for him she seemed not to care.

She accepted his offer of a boat ride,
suggesting she just loved the punt.
John considered he could become an expert,
but his turn of phrase was a little blunt.

So he had to prove his point now,
sort of hoist on his own petard,
John found on those crowded waters
this punting lark is actually quite hard.

They had hardly even got going
when they struck the opposite bank.
He apologised most profusely,
she said as a punter he was pretty rank.

He quickly promised he'd do better.
Thrusting in his pole with enthusiastic vigour.
The blue haired girl just drifted off,
leaving John just hanging above the river!

The Stringer

(for all those in journalism)

It can be a lonely occupation
but most think they're doing quite a job,
representing their small community,
whilst pulling in a good few bob.

There's no doubt some are influential,
for of their home town we hear a lot,
we lift up the national Dailies
to find Clive there six days on the trot.

We've noticed Clive's link with Lyme Regis,
hardly ever it's missing from the news,
its houses, its beaches and the Cob of course,
Clive gaily for us dispensing his latest views.

What's this that has suddenly happened?
Lyme has slipped from the daily reports.
Oh horror the Nation's in mourning
has Lyme dropped in the listing of resorts?

We're asked to refocus our vision,
Cheltenham Spa seems to have taken Lyme's place,
we notice a new name on the tag line,
God forbid that Clive's just slipped from Grace.

Socks

(for all domestic goddesses)

I don't know who invented them
and I can't say that I much care,
but I so wish when I go to the drawer
I could find myself a pair.

I can easily spot the red one
tucked there behind the green,
but where the hell's its partner?
You're right, it's nowhere to be seen.

I think it's all down to Herbert,
that's our machine washer by the way.
When we empty out the washing,
I swear we lose a sock per day.

Now that's not a unique happening,
we've heard others this malaise deplore.
We once did think we were unjust
when a missing sock was behind the door.

I rummage on regardless,
hoping at last I will succeed.
I've found two pairs already,
each unmatched so not what I need.

Success at last, well almost,
A pair of bright blue come to hand.
Will they go well with my dress suit?
Too late now, and certainly not what I planned.

I made a New Year resolution,
we'd pop the socks in one of those bags,
but you know about resolutions,
yep, now we've lost the wretched bags.

If you see me on the High Street,
please don't be alarmed at all,
I've not gone off my trolley,
I don whate'er, so long as not too small.

I do believe a fashion I've started,
odd socks seem acceptable to wear,
it really is quite a blessing,
For now you never can't find a pair.

The Recipe

(for all speciality chefs)

Handed from generation to generation,
secret recipes are known to survive.
Oft time a well kept family secret
created by an ancestor when alive.

Even multinational companies
cherish formulae oh so secret,
they build on these great mysteries,
claiming it's their founder who gets the credit.

Ours was created by Great Great Grandma,
or so the family story goes,
first written down by Mum's Nanna
in a scrawl that now hardly shows.

Finally it became my honoured duty,
to don the Cook's tall hat,
have a crack at the family recipe,
and keep family history on its track.

Alas it didn't work for me.
I followed the letter to the law.
I stirred and beat as instructed
but the inner secret I never saw.

My effort was a disaster,
not fit for mankind to consume.
I checked the faint words once more,
for 'twas my silly error I assume.

I tried again in strictest privacy,
with no one around for the show,
well, it didn't happen this second time,
oh, how my apprehension did grow.

The best I can do to ensure succession,
is to teach a child to have a go,
skip this my failed generation
and hope that the family never know.

Parking

(for the brave public parkers)

I've just completed a long observation,
of parking in various places,
to see why so many poor parkers
come home with miserable faces.

I think few regard their fine motors,
with the respect they surely deserve
and of fellow parkers seem so oblivious,
parking in positions that are frankly absurd.

They squeeze into inappropriate spaces.
Kids fling wide their passenger doors.
The poor car in the next bay shudders.
They walk off without even a pause.

Reversing from well-marked positions,
wheels are turned too early 'tis clear,
bumpers connect with fabulous paintwork,
that frankly was not actually once near.

Carefully selected parking behaviour,
sees parkers scurry to corners far flung,
but God bless me I don't believe it!
. Again they choose my neighbour to become.

Doubtless you've all had the same experience,
no matter how hard we try,
the lack of thought and consideration,
is enough to make a strong person cry.

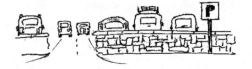

Saturdays

(for the social historians)

It's the day that's undergone most change,
as the years go rolling past.
From a work day when I was a lad,
so many new things have arrived so fast.

For many folks it's still a workday,
selling and providing us with our fun.
The rest of us just have to choose what we do
and enjoy it, come rain or sun.

Sport ranks for many quite highly,
whether playing or cheering from the line.
For others it's just a day of rest
and they don't get up till nine.

Gardens used to be a highlight,
but the fashion is slipping away,
not room for much activity
in the average garden of today.

Now consider the opportunities
laid out at our beck and call,
and without a great deal of expenditure,
if computers don't afflict them all.

Football has a mighty following
despite high prices at the gate.
Clearly not a bar to the multitudes
whose wage or Benefit provide of late.

We hear in the light of Brexit,
a call to return the Saturday job,
so the workers of tomorrow,
can taste work and provide a few bob.

Some enterprising youngsters
of an entrepreneurial bent,
have set up mini businesses
and exploit useful gadgets they invent.

We hear too of a few children,
who volunteer for a spell of caring,
a truly heartening disclosure
and shows we must temper despairing.

So far it's been mostly the day time
that has exercised the mind,
but how about teens to twenties' evenings?
Well I think activities best left behind.

Saturdays will continue changing,
of that we may rest assured,
potential alternatives endless,
but predicting is clearly absurd.

Brexit

(for the apolitical observers)

If you're into odes contemporary,
you'll be surprised not to find one on Brexit.
So here's a few simple observations,
'Cos all Brits just want a pleasant exit.

The Nation received an opportunity
to vote in a democratic way,
canvassing was at times emotive,
but in the end we all had our say.

The balance was not perhaps dramatic,
but clear the Leavers held the day,
the task was now for the Government
and the burden fell entirely on Mrs May.

There was a pause before the start gun sounded,
but by March withdrawal was under way,
the other twenty-seven countries,
scarce believed they'd ever see the day.

Article 50 was duly triggered,
Theresa wrote a letter of six sheets.
Though expected, there were still some shock waves
that echoed around Brussels' streets.

The initial reactions not unexpected,
saw sadness quickly lose its shine.
By day two positions were hardening,
day three 27 formed EU's front line.

The UK was actually a key player,
if for reasons mostly economic,
but to hold the rest of them together
we expect rhetoric that's pretty vitriolic.

Spain is already looking to exploit our leaving,
having another go to recover the Rock.
The EU sees an early opportunity
to exercise protection for its flock.

We clearly will defend Gibraltar,
for that's what a protectorate means,
but it's so clearly symptomatic
and surely just one of the opening scenes.

This ode comes early in the process,
eventually of verses there'll be more,
but meanwhile the most burning issue
is we don't self-destruct, before reaching the door.

2016

Weather Forecasting

(for those that respect folklore)

I've been running through the alphabet,
well actually looking for a theme,
I got right through to W,
when Weather fulfilled my dream.

How could a British person,
for so long have turned his back?
For the UK's known internationally
for its continuous weather chit chat.

I've yet to feel my seaweed,
but I'm sure it's going to rain,
see how close the hills appear,
I'm told from guesswork I should refrain.

That weather App's just wonderful,
so builders and my kids explain,
why keep relying on the seaweed?
Get with it and save our shame.

So I'll leave it to technology
and that lovely weather lady,
to tell me if it's raining outside
or should I seek a place that's shady.

I looked upon my tablet,
saw suns drawn across the board,
I put away the coat and brolly,
went out, guess what? yes it poured.

I drove to the beach last Sunday
to replace my seaweed on the door.
Much as I love that weather lady,
I'll do it the old way to be sure.

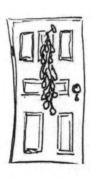

Blended Families

(for the second chancers)

Have you noticed how our language
grows new words and strange new phrases?
If you pay attention to the Media,
daily you'll find a new one that amazes.

My latest is the Blended Family,
a social observation I'm quite sure
but doubtless cunningly descriptive
and daily of such families there's more.

Whether sad or a celebration
of marriages that have failed,
it's good to see new happiness
when partnerships become derailed.

I wonder about the children
when they get caught up in the muddle.
They probably don't have many options
but seem to become befuddled.

We ask they divide their loyalties,
but they 're not the guilty ones,
they mostly love their Mum and Dad
so to adopt new ones, Crumbs!

Of course marriage is decreasingly a factor,
and church vows have lost their meaning,
so to break the union's no worry,
was it founded on boundless feeling?

I'll hide my personal feelings
but doubt I'll be successful,
I know I swim against the tide
for me marriage is nigh perpetual.

Nature intervenes occasionally
and most deserve a second chance,
but when couples break marriage asunder
do children's needs even get a glance?

So we end up with many households
where sex, race, parents, even surname
are stirred up in the melting pot,
but successful so Social Workers claim.

That said, then, Blended Family
seems to fit the bill just fine.
Yes, it is a social definition
but one that well describes our time.

Nostalgia

(for those that relish the past)

Another word that we have borrowed,
I mean Nostos from the Greek.
For them it means to return home,
we added Algia to make the word we seek.

We generally think of looking backwards
to what some believe were better days,
but for others they look but forward,
yesterday for them's just a haze.

For those that do take pleasure
revisiting days long since past,
they draw such satisfaction
and are sure their dreams will last.

Some like me are mostly focussed
on the future and what it holds.
We enjoyed the past but now it's gone
so look ahead as life unfolds.

Of course there is good reason
to remember special things from the past;
mistakes mankind has perpetrated
that must ne'er again be unmasked.

There's a modern oft heard expression
beloved of politicians and many more.
It says that lessons will be learned,
thus saying, it's back to how it was before.

O.K. so I'm just a big cynic,
perhaps things will get turned around,
for now nostalgic glances backwards
are about the good things we have found.

As years roll on, the memories
accumulate by the score.
The old ones last the longest,
until we arrive at Heaven's door.

I think I'm becoming nostalgic.
Nostalgia has grasped my mind.
I've searched deep in my memory
and am full of joy at what I find.

"There was one I didn't agree with, the one about Brexit".

" Well, I liked them all, so there! Anyway, everyone knows no one knows anything about Brexit, especially the Europeans, and you of course".

"Pity about the drawings"

"Let's not go there!"